NATIONAL GEOGRAPHIC

School Publishing

Patterns, Shapes, and Symmetry

Susan Long

PICTURE CREDITS
Cover, 5 (right below), Dorling Kindersley; 1, 4 (left), 8, 9 (left), 10 (right), 12 (below), 13 (right), 14 (right), 15, 17 (left above), 18 (left), 19 (right above), 20, APL/Corbis; 2, 11, Getty Images; 4 (right), John Cancalosi/Nature Picture Library; 5 (right above), 9 (left below), 10 (left), 13 (left), 14 (left), 16, 17 (below left), 18 (right), 19 (below), Photolibrary.com; 6 (left), Jaanus Järva/Alamy; 6 (right), Photofrenetic/Alamy; 7 (above), ImageState/Alamy; 7 (below), JCB-Nature/Alamy; 12 (above), Andrew Lawson Photography/Alamy; 17, Ibis for Kids Australia.

Produced through the worldwide resources of the National Geographic Society, John M. Fahey, Jr., President and Chief Executive Officer; Gilbert M. Grosvenor, Chairman of the Board; Nina D. Hoffman, Executive Vice President and President, Books and Education Publishing Group.

PREPARED BY NATIONAL GEOGRAPHIC SCHOOL PUBLISHING
Steve Mico, Executive Vice President and Publisher, Children's Books and Education Publishing Group; Marianne Hiland, Editor in Chief; Lynnette Brent, Executive Editor; Michael Murphy and Barbara Wood, Senior Editors; Nicole Rouse, Editor; Bea Jackson, Design Director; David Dumo, Art Director; Shanin Glenn, Designer; Margaret Sidlosky, Illustrations Director; Matt Wascavage, Manager of Publishing Services; Sean Philpotts, Production Manager.

MANUFACTURING AND QUALITY MANAGEMENT
Christopher A. Liedel, Chief Financial Officer; Phillip L. Schlosser, Vice President; Clifton M. Brown III, Director.

BOOK DEVELOPMENT
Ibis for Kids Australia Pty Limited.

Published by the National Geographic Society
1145 17th Street, N.W.
Washington, D.C. 20036-4688

Product No. 4W1005059

ISBN-13: 978-1-4263-5055-9
ISBN-10: 1-4263-5055-4

2010 2009 2008 2007 2006
1 2 3 4 5 6 7 8 9 10 11 12 13 14 15

Printed in China

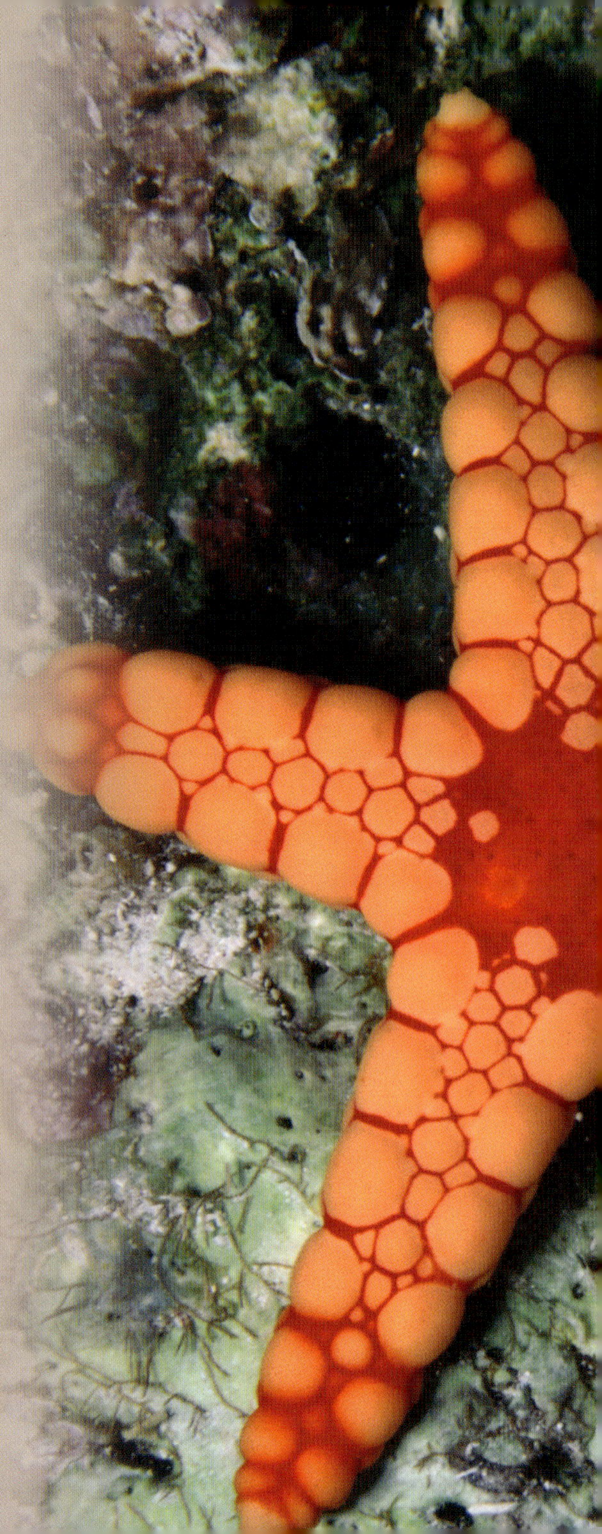

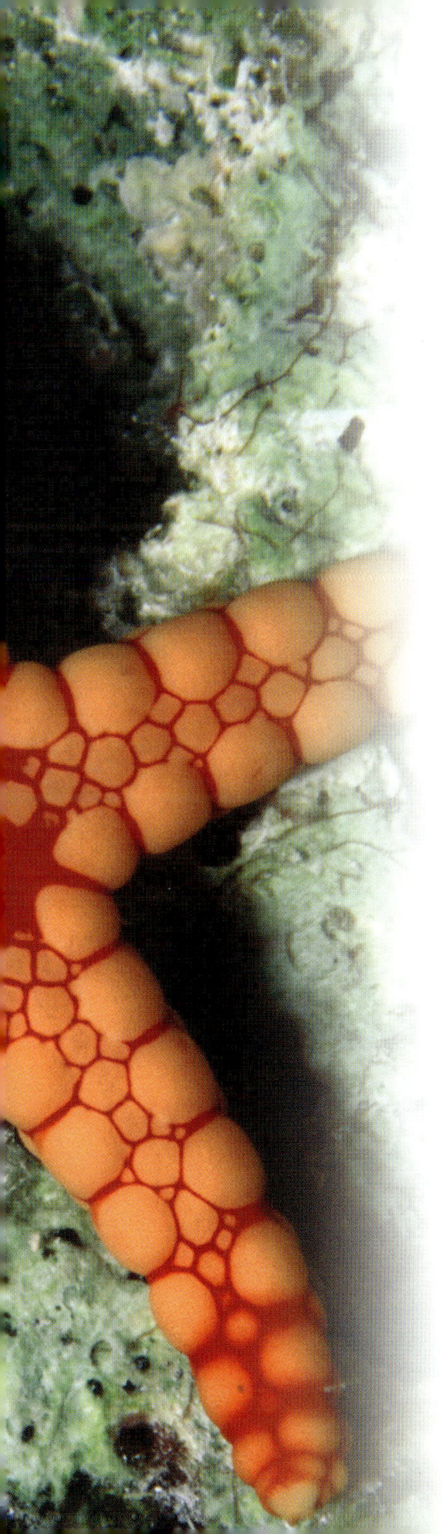

Contents

Think and Discuss

beach tents

seashell

What patterns do you see in these pictures? What shapes do you see?

Patterns Are All Around You

There are **patterns** in nature.
A pattern has two or more parts, or pieces, that repeat over and over.

Look at the red stripe, black stripe pattern on this bug.

Look at the patterns on this fish.

Look at the patterns on this tortoise shell.

Look at the patterns on these leaves.

There are patterns in things made by people.

You can find patterns on clothing.

You can find patterns on tablecloths.

You can find patterns on floors.

Other Patterns

There are many other kinds of patterns you can make. For example, you can make sound patterns.

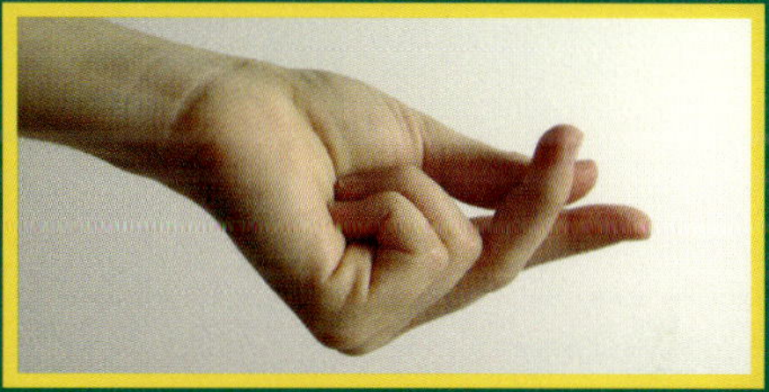

Snap

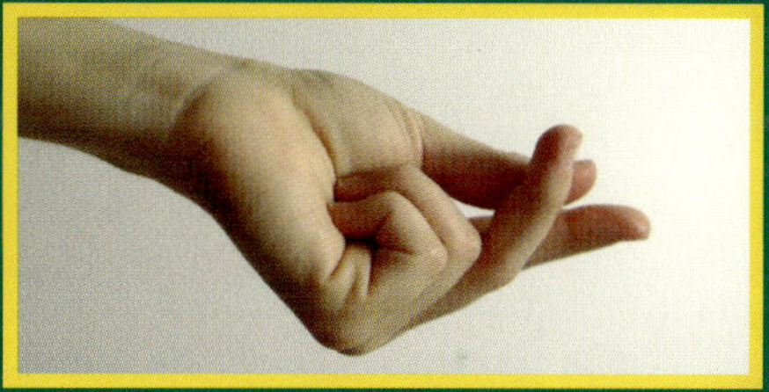

Snap

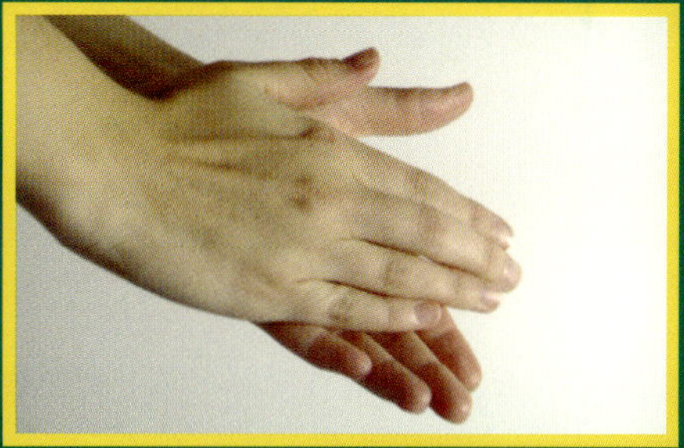

Clap

If you repeat snap, snap, clap; snap, snap, clap, you make a sound pattern.

Shapes Are All Around You

There are **shapes** in nature.

The leaves on this fern are shaped like **triangles**.

The hole in this tree is shaped like a **circle**.

There are many shapes
on this sea star.

There are shapes in things made by people.

This pool of water is shaped like a **square**.

The sides of most buildings are shaped like **rectangles**.

These sails are shaped like triangles.

Shapes in Design

Shapes can be used to create designs. Both of these quilts were made using shapes.

Symmetry Is All Around You

Some things have **symmetry**.
This means they have two sides that match.
Some things in nature have symmetry.

giraffe

maple leaf

The dotted line is a **line of symmetry**. It helps us see that one **half** matches the other half.

butterfly

sand dollar

There is symmetry in things made by people.

the Taj Mahal, a famous building in India

Make Your Own Symmetry

1 Fold a paper square into a triangle as many times as you can.

2 Cut out notches (triangles or other shapes) along the edges.

3 Open up the paper. You have made a beautiful snowflake!

Use What You Learned

Where can you see patterns in these pictures?
Where can you see shapes and symmetry?

beach umbrella

zebra

circle

half

line of symmetry

pattern

rectangle

shape

square

symmetry

triangle

Picture Glossary

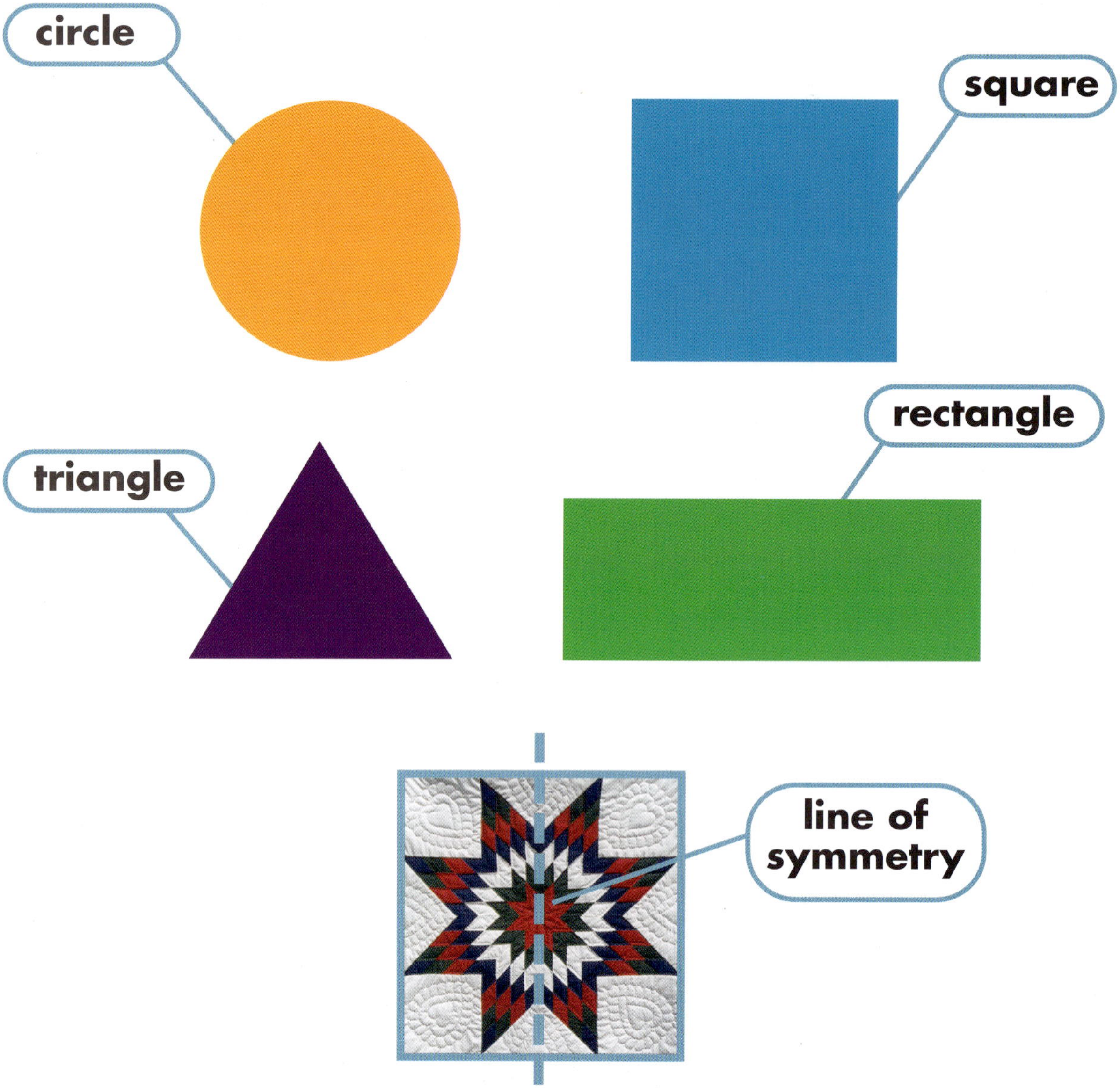